THE MILLIONAIRE'S WEEKEND PLAYBOOK: STRATEGIES FOR RAPID WEALTH ACCUMULATION

WENDY A. JOHNSON

Table Of Contents

Introduction

Welcome to "The Millionaire's Weekend Playbook: Strategies for Rapid Wealth Accumulation." In the high speed universe of money, the excursion to tycoon status requires key preparation, restrained execution, and a mentality designed for progress. This playbook is your manual for exploring the intricacies of abundance amassing, offering functional experiences, noteworthy stages, and tried and true methodologies to speed up your monetary excursion. Whether you're a carefully prepared financial backer or simply beginning, this book means to engage you with the instruments expected to settle on informed choices and fabricate an enduring tradition of thriving. Let the establishing long term financial stability venture start!

Chapter 1

Setting the Foundation

In this section, "Setting the Foundation," we set out on the pivotal period of laying out a versatile base for your monetary excursion. The part unfurls in two key segments:

- Creating a Stable Financial Foundation:

This segment digs into the centre standards of developing a strong monetary establishment. Understanding the significance of a hearty base is key to supporting monetary achievement. You'll learn practical ways to improve your financial standing, such as developing smart saving habits and structuring a diversified portfolio.

- Management of expenses and a budget:

Inside this subsection, the centre goes to the careful craft of planning and overseeing costs actually. Acquire experiences into making a reasonable spending plan that lines up with your monetary objectives, and find down to earth ways to deal with smooth out and improve your costs. Dominating these abilities guarantees that your monetary base isn't simply strong yet versatile to the powerful scene of abundance gathering.

Together, these parts structure the foundation of your monetary design, making way for the establishing financial stability methodologies to come. As you go through "Setting the Foundation," equip yourself with the knowledge and tools you need to build a solid financial foundation that lasts.

Chapter 2

Investing Wisely
In the second section, "Investing Wisely," the centre movements to the workmanship and study of astute financial planning. This urgent phase of your monetary excursion includes the accompanying segments:

- Broadening Your Portfolio:
Investigate the meaning of enhancement in ventures. Comprehend how spreading your ventures across different resource classes can moderate dangers and streamline returns. Gain proficiency with the standards behind making an even and differentiated portfolio custom-made to your monetary objectives.

- Procedures for Fruitful Ventures:

Dive into demonstrated systems for making educated and effective ventures. From market examination to gambling with the board, this segment gives noteworthy experiences into exploring the intricacies of the speculation scene. Furnish yourself with the devices to settle on essential venture choices lined up with your abundance gathering targets.

Chapter 2 fills in as a manual for exploring the unique universe of speculations, guaranteeing that you settle on informed decisions to improve your monetary development.

Chapter 3

Income Generation
In the third part, "Income Generation," the centre moves towards investigating roads for expanding your pay. This part involves the accompanying areas:

- Investigating Extra Revenue Sources:

Find the significance of differentiating your pay sources past conventional channels. Investigate different open doors, like side gigs, independent work, or automated sources of income, to enhance and upgrade your generally acquiring potential. All of these can add to your Income along side consistency and reduction of negativity.

- Pioneering Adventures and Second jobs:

Dive into the universe of business and part time jobs. Learn how to effectively manage side projects, start profitable businesses, and identify viable business opportunities. This segment gives bits of knowledge into transforming your enthusiasm or abilities into productive revenue sources.

Chapter 3 engages you to proactively grow your kinds of revenue, cultivating monetary versatility and speeding up your excursion towards abundance amassing.

Chapter 4

Real Estate Ventures

In the fourth segment, "Real estate Ventures," the middle developments to the potential developing long haul monetary security significant entryways inside the area of land. This part consolidates the going with regions:

- Helping Returns through Property: Examine strategies for amplifying land venture returns. Handle the principles of property decision, market examination, and strong organisation to ensure your territory undertakings contribute out and out to your overflow assortment. Splendid Land

- Hypothesis Techniques:

Dive into wise and key ways of managing land adventure. From recognizing creating business areas to investigating supporting decisions, this section gives huge encounters to making informed decisions in the strong land scene.

Chapter 4 outlines how to use land's potential as an essential component of your system for gathering wealth. Sort out some way to investigate the intricacies of the property hypothesis and position yourself for financial accomplishment.

Chapter 5

Savings and Emergency Funds

In the fifth section, "Savings and Emergency Funds," the emphasis is on the significance of monetary wellbeing nets and restrained saving. This part includes the accompanying segments:

- How Emergency Funds Help:
Comprehending the basic job of crisis subsidises monetary security. Figure out how to lay out and keep a backup stash to shield against unanticipated costs, guaranteeing your monetary security stays strong.

- Planned Savings That Work:
Investigate reasonable and successful reserve funds plans custom fitted to your monetary objectives. From transient

targets to long haul yearnings, this segment gives experiences into organizing investment funds designs that line up with your abundance collection system.

You'll learn how to strategically save money and build financial buffers in Chapter 5, two crucial steps on your way to rapid wealth accumulation.

Chapter 6

Retirement Planning
In the 6th part, "Retirement Planning," the center movements to getting your monetary future during retirement. This part envelops the accompanying segments:

- Getting Your Future:
Recognize the significance of thorough retirement planning. Investigate different retirement reserve funds vehicles and venture methodologies to guarantee a monetarily secure and agreeable retirement.

- Retirement Speculation Techniques:
Dig into viable speculation methodologies explicitly customised for retirement. Figure out how to adjust chance and return, advance your retirement portfolio,

and pursue informed choices to help your post-vocation way of life.

Part 6 fills in as your manual for exploring the intricacies of retirement arranging, guaranteeing that your abundance gathering venture reaches out into a protected and satisfying retirement stage.

Chapter 7

Tax Optimization
In the seventh section, "Assessment Improvement," the attention is on limiting expense liabilities and boosting your abundance through essential duty arranging. This part involves the accompanying areas:

- Limiting Duty Liabilities:
Investigate compelling methodologies to limit taxation rates lawfully. You can save more of your hard-earned money by taking advantage of tax deductions, credits, and incentives that align with your financial objectives.

- Charge Proficient Speculation Techniques:

Investigate investment strategies that are made to be as tax-efficient as possible. Find out how to structure your investments to minimise taxable income, maximise returns, and navigate the tax regulations' ever-evolving landscape.

Chapter 7 furnishes you with the information to explore the complexities of the expense framework, guaranteeing that you proactively deal with your assessment commitments and save a greater amount of your abundance for sped up gathering.

Chapter 8

Mindset and Discipline

In the eighth section, "Mindset and Discipline," the centre movements to the mental perspectives significant for supported monetary achievement. This part involves the accompanying areas:

- Fostering a Growing long term financial stability Outlook:

Investigate the mindset that is necessary for accumulating wealth over time. Comprehend the job of positive reasoning, objective setting, and steadiness in defeating monetary difficulties and accomplishing your abundance goals.

- The Job of Discipline in Monetary Achievement:

Dive into the significance of discipline in monetary administration. Figure out how to develop propensities that advance monetary discipline, guaranteeing consistency in your way to deal with planning, effective money management, and in general growing a strong financial foundation.

Chapter 8 fills in as a manual for developing the psychological backbone and discipline expected to explore the promising and less promising times of your monetary excursion, at last adding to supported and sped up abundance gathering.

Chapter 9

Review and Adjust

The ninth chapter, "Review and Adjust," focuses on your financial strategies' ongoing evaluation and adaptation. This part includes the accompanying areas:

- Customary Monetary Designated spots:

Grasp the significance of leading standard evaluations of your monetary wellbeing. Find out how to set up checkpoints to review your financial goals, investments, and overall plan to make sure they are in line with your changing priorities.

- Adjusting Techniques to Market Changes:

Explore methods for coping with shifting market conditions. Comprehend how to change your monetary methodologies in light of financial movements, guaranteeing versatility and proceed with progress towards your abundance gathering objectives.

Chapter 9 aides you through the course of consistent assessment and change, encouraging adaptability and flexibility in your monetary methodology for supported achievement.

Conclusion

In the closing part, we unite the vital bits of knowledge and techniques examined in "The Millionaire's Weekend Playbook: Strategies For Rapid Wealth Accumulation." This segment fills in as an exhaustive rundown, underscoring the significance of a balanced way to deal with monetary achievement.

Think about the standards of sound monetary administration, trained money management, and proactive preparation. The end urges you to apply the procured information to your interesting monetary conditions, cultivating an outlook intended for long haul thriving.

As you finish this playbook, think of it as an aide as well as an impetus for groundbreaking change in your monetary life. Outfitted with these techniques, set out on your excursion with certainty and reason, realising that your way to abundance aggregation is currently obvious.